CW00369730

INDIAN OCEAN

AUSTRALIA

NEW
ZEALAND

SOUTHERN OCEAN

ANTARCTICA

PENGUINS

PENGUINS

LIFESTYLE • HABITAT • FEEDING • BEHAVIOUR

DANIEL GILPIN

PaRragon

Bath · New York · Singapore · Hong Kong · Cologne · Delhi · Melbourne

First published by Parragon in 2009

Parragon
Queen Street House
4 Queen Street
Bath BA1 1HE, UK

Copyright © Parragon Books Ltd 2007

Designed, produced and packaged by Stonecastle Graphics Limited

Text by Daniel Gilpin
Designed by Sue Pressley and Paul Turner
Edited by Philip de Ste. Croix
Illustrations by William Donohoe

All rights reserved. No part of this publication may be reproduced,
stored in a retrieval system, or transmitted in any way or by any
means, electronic, mechanical, photocopying, recording or otherwise,
without the prior permission of the copyright holder.

ISBN 978-1-4075-7679-4

Printed in China

Contents

The Penguin

Penguins are everything a bird should not be. They are creatures that spend most of their time in or under the water, and absolutely none of it up in the air. They are plump, noisy, flightless and clumsy on land. And yet they are successful. Penguins are masters of the Antarctic ice and divers without parallel in the bird kingdom. They are also surprisingly widespread. Some species are far more at home in the heat of the tropical sun than they would be in the frozen wastes far to the south.

What is a Penguin?

Penguins are birds adapted for life in the sea. They have lost the power of flight and become masters of swimming, with streamlined bodies shaped like torpedoes to cut easily through the water. Unlike other birds, penguins cannot bend their wings in the middle. Instead, these limbs have become stiff paddles, with the bones inside them fused together for strength.

Penguins are extremely powerful swimmers and can move through the water with surprising speed. The fastest, the Gentoo Penguin (*Pygoscelis papua*), can reach 17mph (27kph) in short bursts and most species regularly exceed 15mph (24kph). As well as being fast swimmers, penguins are extremely manoeuvrable in the water, using their webbed feet and tails as rudders to make sharp turns as they chase after prey.

In the water, penguins are a vision of power and grace. On land, however, they can appear almost comical in their attempts to get about. Their feet are set so far back on their bodies that they are forced to stand upright in order to move, giving them a vaguely human appearance. The alternative, in snow at least, is to 'toboggan' on their bellies, using their clawed feet to push them along.

There have been penguins on Earth for an extremely long time. The oldest known penguin fossils date back 55 million years and many scientists believe that they evolved even earlier than this. By contrast, our own species has only existed for around 120,000 years. The earliest known human ancestors first came down from the trees and stood upright just over four million years ago.

Above: Penguins walk upright because their feet are set so far back on their bodies. This gives them a comical, almost human appearance.

Right: In the water, penguins use their feet as rudders. They effortlessly propel themselves through the water with their stiff, paddle-like wings.

Left: Penguins are closely related to albatrosses. In a few places the two share nesting sites, as here in the Falkland Islands. This mixed colony contains Rockhopper Penguins and Black-browed Albatrosses.

Below: Chinstrap Penguins use icebergs as convenient, safe places to rest between fishing trips in the cold waters of the Southern Ocean.

Perhaps surprisingly, the closest living relatives of the penguins are the albatrosses, which include many of the world's largest flying birds. The Wandering Albatross, which shares the Southern Ocean with several penguin species, has a wingspan of up to 12ft (3.7m), the greatest of any bird alive today. Other birds more closely resemble penguins, however. In the northern hemisphere, auks, which include puffins, guillemots and razorbills, have evolved along similar lines to fill a similar ecological niche. Like penguins, which are confined to the southern hemisphere, they hunt fish by chasing them under water. There was even one species, the Great Auk, that was flightless. It was hunted to extinction in the 19th century.

Penguins are well adapted for cold conditions. Their rounded bodies have few extremities through which heat can be lost and those they do possess have their own adaptations to conserve heat. The blood vessels

extending into penguins' feet, for example, run alongside those carrying blood back from the feet into the body, allowing heat to be exchanged between the two. Cold blood returning from the toes is warmed by hot blood coming from the body. A similar system operates in the wings.

Beneath the skin, penguins have a thick layer of blubber that acts both as a food store and insulation to help keep them warm. Penguin feathers are very small, densely packed and heavily oiled. They also help to conserve heat, but more importantly reduce drag in the water. Penguins are unique among birds in being such powerful swimmers that they can actually leap right out of the water while on the move. Known as 'porpoising', this manoeuvre enables them to grab a breath without having to slow down. It is also an important escape tactic, helping to confuse predators that are chasing them under water.

Above: Penguins have streamlined, teardrop-shaped bodies and sleek feathers, as these Gentoos clearly show.

Penguins are among the most sociable of all birds, breeding, travelling and feeding in large flocks. When moving across ice, penguins often walk, but they also toboggan, sliding on their bellies while pushing themselves along with their feet. These are Adélie Penguins, a common sight all around Antarctica.

Penguin Types

There are 17 different species of penguin. Scientists split them up into six different groups, known as genera (singular: genus). All living things are classified using a two-part scientific Latin name. The first part of that name identifies the genus, while the second part is unique to the species.

The largest and second-largest species of penguin, the Emperor and King Penguins, belong to the genus *Aptenodytes*. They differ from other penguins not only in size but also in coloration and shape of the bill. Both Emperor (*Aptenodytes forsteri*) and King Penguins (*Aptenodytes patagonicus*) have long, pointed bills with an orange stripe along the bottom mandible. They also have yellowy-orange patches behind the eyes and a slightly less intensely coloured bib on the front of the neck. The Emperor Penguin is the larger of the two, weighing up to 84lb (38kg) and measuring 45in (115cm) from bill tip to tail. The King Penguin reaches 37½in (95cm) in length but weighs less than half as much as the Emperor, rarely exceeding 35lb (16kg). It can also be distinguished by the lighter grey feathers it has on its back.

The Yellow-eyed Penguin, has the distinction of being in a genus of its own; *Megadyptes* (*Megadyptes antipodes*). The Royal Penguin is one of six species in the genus *Eudyptes*, commonly known as the crested penguins. As the name suggests, crested penguins can be easily identified by their yellow crests, which extend from the head like huge eyebrows. The black feathers on top of a crested penguin's head are also longer than those in other penguins and can be raised for display. As well as the Royal Penguin (*Eudyptes schlegeli*), crested penguins include the Macaroni Penguin (*Eudyptes chrysolophus*), the Fjordland Penguin (*Eudyptes pachyrhynchus*), the Rockhopper Penguin (*Eudyptes chrysocome*), the Snares Penguin (*Eudyptes robustus*) and the Erect-crested Penguin (*Eudyptes sclateri*).

Perhaps the most familiar of all penguins are those that belong to the banded group, as they tend to be the most commonly kept penguins in zoos. There are four species of banded penguin that make up the *Spheniscus* genus: the African or Jackass Penguin (*Spheniscus demersus*), the Galápagos Penguin (*Spheniscus mendiculus*), the Magellanic Penguin (*Spheniscus magellanicus*) and the Humboldt Penguin (*Spheniscus humboldti*). Banded penguins have dark grey or black faces with white 'eyebrows', which extend

Right: The King Penguin is the second largest of all penguin species: only the Emperor Penguin is bigger. King Penguins have much lighter feathers on their backs than Emperors and more vivid orange patches behind their ears.

around to the front of the neck. They also have dark bands and occasional spots of feathers on their otherwise glowing white bellies.

Three species make up the genus *Pygoscelis*. The Adélie Penguin (*Pygoscelis adeliae*), Chinstrap Penguin (*Pygoscelis antarctica*) and Gentoo Penguins (*Pygoscelis papua*) are better known as the brush-tailed penguins. Unlike most other penguins, which have stumpy but neat, fleshy tails, brush-tailed penguins have long, stiff feathers sticking out from the back.

The last of the six penguin genera, *Eudyptula*, is another that contains just one species, the Fairy or Little Penguin (*Eudyptula minor*), which is also sometimes known as the Blue Penguin. As its name suggests, the Fairy Penguin is the smallest of all penguin species, reaching just 16 1/2in (42cm) in length and weighing no more than 3lb (1.3kg).

Above: The crested penguins are the punk rockers of the bird world, sporting colourful, if sometimes unkempt-looking, head-dresses of feathers. Despite its name, this species, the Erect-crested Penguin, often lets its crest feathers droop down by its neck.

Left: The Fairy Penguin is the smallest penguin of all and the only one to nest on mainland Australia. Despite its diminutive size, it has a surprisingly powerful voice. Birds at their breeding colonies are particularly vocal, making a cacophonous variety of loud quacking, braying and whistling noises.

Right: The Gentoo is the largest of the three brush-tailed penguin species and the third largest of all penguins, after the Emperor and King. Gentoos have a distinctive white stripe that stretches across the top of the head and are the only brush-tailed penguins with an orange bill.

Below: Compared with other penguins, Emperor Penguins are huge. The males in particular put on a massive amount of weight in the run-up to winter in preparation for months of starvation while they incubate their partners' eggs out on the ice.

Left: The Yellow-eyed Penguin has a genus all of its own. It has the unhappy distinction of being the world's rarest penguin, with fewer than 4000 individual birds remaining. It is found only on New Zealand and a few outlying islands.

Left: Unlike New Zealand's Yellow-eyed penguin, the Chinstrap is thriving. The second most common of all penguins, it has a population that numbers in the millions and is found right around Antarctica.

Opposite: The Magellanic Penguin is the most common of the four banded penguin species, breeding right around the southern tip of South America. Like all of the banded penguins, it has characteristic white 'eyebrows' of feathers and a flattened bill.

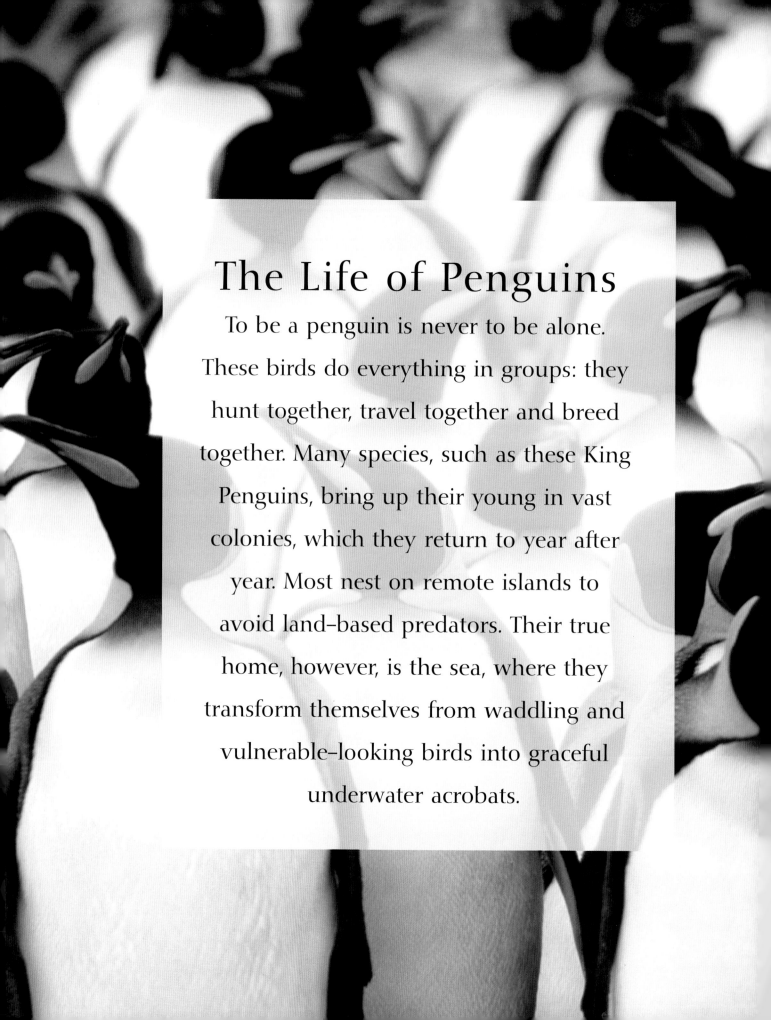

The Life of Penguins

To be a penguin is never to be alone. These birds do everything in groups: they hunt together, travel together and breed together. Many species, such as these King Penguins, bring up their young in vast colonies, which they return to year after year. Most nest on remote islands to avoid land–based predators. Their true home, however, is the sea, where they transform themselves from waddling and vulnerable–looking birds into graceful underwater acrobats.

Food and Feeding

Penguins are diving birds that find all their food in the sea. Their entire diet is made up of three different animal groups: fish, squid and crustaceans. The relative balance between these three is dictated partly by where the different species of penguin live and also by slight differences in the techniques they use to capture prey.

Before we look in depth at the various hunting techniques penguins use, it is sensible first to consider their prey. In the Southern Ocean around Antarctica fish can be surprisingly hard to find. Despite the enormous size of this marine ecosystem, it is home to just 120 different fish species – an incredibly low number considering that there are more than 25,000 species of fish worldwide. Part of the reason for this paucity of species is the relative depth of the Southern Ocean. While the sea immediately surrounding most land masses in the world averages about 425ft (130m) in depth, that around Antarctica averages 1650ft (500m). The shallow areas that elsewhere provide important nursery grounds for young fish are almost absent here. Antarctic fish tend either to congregate near the bottom or to live in small numbers immediately under the ice. For this reason, they make up only a small part of the diets of most Antarctic penguins.

While fish are scarce in Antarctic waters, the shrimp-like crustaceans known as krill exist here in vast numbers. One species more than any other underpins the Antarctic food chain. *Euphausia superba* – a type of krill measuring around 2 1/2in (6cm) in length commonly known as Antarctic krill – lives in open water where it forms dense shoals, sometimes of staggering proportions. The largest shoal ever measured was over 650ft (200m) deep and spread across an area of 60 square miles (155km²). It was estimated to contain around 10 million tons of krill, or 5 trillion (5000 billion) individual animals. Most shoals of krill are much smaller than this, typically covering less than 720 square yards (600m²). Even so, they contain massive amounts of prey and draw penguins and other predators over long distances to feed on them.

Although they inhabit open water, krill tend to avoid the shallows whenever possible during the day, rising up through the water column at

---

Right: Adélies enter the water one after the other in quick succession, like members of a synchronized diving team. These penguins feed primarily on krill, shrimp-like crustaceans that form vast swarms in the surface waters of the Southern Ocean around Antarctica.

night to feed on the phytoplankton (photosynthetic algae) that thrive at the surface. This makes them difficult for many air-breathing creatures to reach, but not for penguins, which have become master divers.

The fact that krill usually lie beyond the reach of flying sea birds explains their relative rarity in the Southern Ocean compared with penguins. In terms of biomass (combined body weight), penguins outnumber other birds in this region by more than 65 to 1. In other words, for every 4lb (1.8kg) of bird flesh in the Southern Ocean, all but 1oz (28g) comes from a penguin.

Farther north, krill become less common and fish stocks increase. Along the coasts of South America and Southern Africa in particular, penguins feed mainly on sardines, pilchards and anchovies, which gather there in vast shoals. Galápagos Penguins also rely on fish for the bulk of their diet, hunting small, shoaling fish such as sardines and mullet.

Squid are taken by most penguins when the chance arises but two species, the King and Emperor Penguins, specialize in hunting them. These large penguins are the greatest divers of all, plunging to enormous depths to

Right: The King Penguin is a deep water specialist that feeds mainly on squid. Its bill is longer than that of most other penguins, an adaptation to help it catch this slightly larger prey.

Opposite: Magellanic Penguins migrate north for the winter, following the movements of the shoals of fish on which they feed. Those that breed on South America's Pacific coast may travel as far north as Peru.

Below: African Penguins nest all year round and rarely stray far from their breeding colonies. Like all penguins, they enter and leave the water in groups for reasons of safety.

reach the places where squid shoals are common. King Penguins have been known to dive as deep as 1065ft (325m) in search of food. Emperors frequently go even deeper: the record dive for a tagged Emperor Penguin was measured at 1870ft (565m). Perhaps unsurprisingly this was the deepest dive ever recorded for any bird. Emperor Penguins can stay under water for up to 18 minutes at a time. They manage this feat by slowing their heart rates and reducing the flow of blood to areas where it is not needed, thus making the most of the oxygen that it contains. All penguins have blood that is extremely rich in haemoglobin, the substance in the blood corpuscles that carries oxygen. They also have high concentrations of myoglobin in their muscle tissues, where oxygen is most needed during dives. Like haemoglobin, myoglobin holds oxygen to be released when it is required. It is topped up whenever a penguin breathes.

Like all birds, penguins lay their eggs and raise their young on land (or, in the case of the Emperor Penguin, ice). They are also forced to spend between two and six weeks of the year on land while they moult, growing new feathers to replace their old, battered ones. Most of a penguin's life, however, is spent at sea – as much as 75 per cent in some species. When they are not hunting food, they are travelling in search of new feeding sites or resting at the surface.

The life of penguins at sea is still shrouded in many mysteries. Scientists are unsure, for example, exactly how they locate shoals of fish and other food in open water and how they navigate to and from their breeding colonies. A few species effectively disappear for parts of the year, with no one being certain where they travel when they are not breeding.

What is known is that some penguins travel farther than others. Emperor Penguins are the greatest wanderers, often staying at sea for months at a time. During these stints they may travel more than 900 miles (1500km) from their breeding grounds. King Penguins also range widely but generally stay within 300 miles (500km) or so of the place where they nest.

Smaller penguins tend to travel shorter distances from land. When they have young to feed, all species make relatively short forays, rarely staying away for more than a couple of days at a time. During these trips they may travel 30 miles (50km) or so before returning. Penguins that generally hunt close to the shore, such as Yellow-eyed Penguins and Gentoos, usually make their round trips in less than 12 hours.

Unlike some sea birds, which bring back food for their young in their beaks, penguins swallow their catch and carry it back in their stomachs. When they return, they regurgitate half-digested food for their chicks.

Penguins rely principally on their eyesight to find food. For those species that hunt relatively near the surface by day this poses no obvious problems, but scientists have long been puzzling how penguins follow their prey at depth or when hunting at night, as some Chinstrap and Macaroni Penguins do. The answer, it seems, lies in the nature of their prey. Most squid, fish and krill caught by penguins in deep water or at night have luminous

Left: When returning to shallow sloping shores many penguins, such as these Gentoos, ride in on breaking waves like surfers.

Above: Penguin chicks stimulate their parents to regurgitate food. The chicks of most species grow fast and require frequent meals until they fledge.

Left: Beneath the water penguins are swift and agile hunters. Their flexible necks enable them to follow even the tightest turns of escaping prey. This African Penguin has the stubby, flattened bill of a species adapted for hunting fish.

organs or glowing spots scattered over their bodies. They produce light in order to communicate with one another in the dark, but in doing so they unwittingly draw penguins and other visual predators towards them.

Unusually among birds, penguins can swallow under water. This enables them to catch more than one prey item per dive – an important ability for birds that feed on shoaling animals and particularly for those that make deep dives in order to find food. The sea water that penguins swallow with their prey means that they ingest high levels of salt. This is expelled from the body via glands beneath the skin above each eye which drain into the nasal cavity. When a penguin emerges from the sea after hunting, drops of salty liquid run from its nostrils and drip off the end of its beak.

Catching fish or squid is difficult but penguins are supremely adapted for the job. Not only are they able to turn suddenly to follow the movements of their prey but they can twist their heads to snap it up even when it makes a last-ditch change of direction. When swimming at speed, a penguin hunches its head into its shoulders to make it more streamlined but, when hunting, its flexible neck comes into its own.

Observations of penguins under water have shown that they tend to attack prey from below. This is partly because it is easier to see a target silhouetted against the light streaming down from above and partly because the prey is less able to escape to deeper water where the penguins might be unable to follow. This method of penguin attack also helps to explain their coloration. Their dark backs make it harder for prey to spot them as they circle below. Similarly, their light bellies make it more difficult for creatures that hunt them to pick them out when attacking from below. This split coloration is known as counter-shading and is common among sea creatures, including other sea birds.

Above: Between dives to catch fish, penguins rest with their heads and backs above the surface. These birds are naturally buoyant and bob up as soon as their wings stop beating. Diving takes some effort but these rests enable them to recover their strength quickly.

Opposite: Emperor Penguins bring up their young sometimes miles from the water's edge. Each hunting trip to provide food for the chick requires a long trek across the ice before it can even begin. To speed up the long journey to the sea they will often toboggan along on their bellies.

Nesting and Young

Most penguins breed once a year. Although the exact timing and behaviour does vary between species, the general pattern is for adult males to arrive first at the breeding colonies in late spring. Upon arrival, they set about building a nest, or refurbishing the one they used the year before. By virtue of where they live and the fact that they cannot fly, penguin nests tend to be simple affairs made from locally available material. Some, such as Adélie Penguins, create nests from pebbles and others from grass. Many nest on open scrapes in the ground or, where the ground is soft enough, dig burrows. Male Emperor and King Penguins fail to build nests at all, as they incubate the eggs while they are balanced on top of their feet.

Once a male penguin has claimed a nest site, he begins to advertise the fact by calling loudly. Penguin calls are perhaps the least melodious of all bird sounds. The cacophonies created by colonies of advertising males have been variously described as sounding like fields full of donkeys all braying together, or like thousands of wheelbarrows with squeaky wheels all being pushed at once.

Each penguin species makes its own distinctive racket, which can be heard from some distance. While it may grate on our ears, it imparts important information to the females, who arrive at the breeding colonies a few days after the males. They use the calls to help them select a mate, although exactly what they look for in the riot of sounds is unclear. Interestingly, the majority end up choosing the males with which they mated the previous year, although not all females remain faithful, with some selecting new partners. Penguins breeding for the first time shed a little more light on this mystery, with females tending to choose males with deeper calls. These males tend to be larger than their rivals and so, presumably, better able to defend the nest from interlopers and provide food for the chicks.

Once pairs have formed, they strengthen their mutual bond by means of ritualized displays. Individual penguins are quite aggressive birds but most courtship rituals involve appearing as unintimidating as possible, hiding bills, exposing vulnerable areas of the body and indulging in appeasement

Right: The Adélie nests farther south than any other penguin species, following the retreating ice sheet to its southernmost limits in spring. As a result, the Adélie breeding season is relatively short. Less than five months pass between pairs mating and their chicks fledging and leaving the colony before the sea ice returns.

Left: A pair of Gentoo Penguins greet one another at the nest as one partner returns from fishing to take over incubation duties. Calling like this reinforces the pair bond. Gentoos incubate their eggs for around 34 days.

Opposite: African Penguins build their nests from whatever material is available, in this case sticks. In some colonies these penguins excavate burrows but in others they nest in depressions on the surface, sheltered by boulders or bushes.

displays, such as bowing. Penguin pairs also vocalize together and many mutually preen. Once the bond between them has been cemented, they also work together on looking after and improving the nest. This often involves stealing pebbles or other material from absent or dozing neighbours. Frequently the thieves get away with their crime, but if they are caught in the act, it usually leads to a fight, although these are rarely serious.

A penguin colony is a busy place. Most species that nest on the ground, such as Chinstrap Penguins, build their nests so that their occupants are just out of pecking range of one another. Burrowers, such as Magellanic Penguins, have a bit more privacy but even they nest in relatively close proximity. Breeding colonies are used again and again, often over centuries. Carbon-dating has shown that some Adélie Penguin colonies have been occupied for more than 4000 years.

Most penguins nest in colonies close to the sea but some go a little way inland to breed. In New Zealand, Yellow-eyed Penguins waddle right across the beach and into the forests, where they nest in burrows amid the roots of the moss-covered trees. On South Georgia east of the Falkland Islands Macaroni Penguins climb for an hour and a half to reach their bustling colony. Chinstrap Penguins on Deception Island at the tip of the Antarctic Peninsula go through an even greater challenge to reach their nests. After leaving the sea, they clamber up huge slopes of volcanic ash criss-crossed with meltwater torrents to their rookery. Its top edge is more than a quarter of a mile (400m) above sea level and is frequently covered by clouds.

Opposite: Rockhopper pairs return to the same nest site year after year, tidying up and refurbishing their nests before laying. This species has one of the widest breeding ranges of any penguin with colonies right around the sub-Antarctic, from the tip of South America to islands south of Australia and New Zealand.

The longest journeys, however, are made by Adélie and Emperor Penguins, which walk for miles across the Antarctic sea ice to the place where they lay their eggs. As the southern spring turns to summer, the sea ice gradually melts, so that by the time the chicks are ready to make their first forays into the Southern Ocean, it is virtually on their doorstep.

Female penguins lay their eggs a few days after mating. Most species lay two eggs, the exceptions being King and Emperor Penguins, which lay one. Incubation lasts between around one to two months. Smaller penguins have shorter incubation periods – the Fairy Penguin sits on its eggs for around 33 days before they hatch. At the other end of the scale Emperor Penguins incubate theirs for 64 days. Both parents take turns with incubation duties, apart from Emperor Penguins, where the egg is cared for solely by the male.

Penguin eggs have unusually thick shells to compensate for the clumsiness of their parents, but this makes hatching very hard work. As with most birds, a hatching penguin chick gets no assistance from its parents. It may tap away at the inside of the shell with its egg tooth – a

short, sharp spike on the end of its beak – for hours before it makes even a crack. The cracking process then continues for anything up to three days before the chick finally breaks out and its egg tooth drops off.

Feeding the young is a job normally undertaken by both parents. While one is away fishing, the other stays with the nest and its brood. As is often the way with penguins, however, there are exceptions to this rule. Among crested penguins, the males stay at the nest and guard the young while the females alone go to sea and bring back food. Emperor Penguins have a unique system of their own, as we will discover later.

Although most penguins lay two eggs, it not uncommon for them only to be successful in raising one chick or, indeed, failing to raise any at all. Egg thieves abound around penguin colonies, with gulls, skuas and other scavenging sea birds quick to pounce on any unguarded nest. Small chicks are also vulnerable if left unattended, and both eggs and chicks are sometimes crushed on beaches shared with Southern Elephant Seals.

The greatest risk of all to penguin chicks is starvation. In a year when food stocks are plentiful, most pairs will successfully raise two young. In

Above: The Chinstrap Penguin is one of just four species to nest on the Antarctic continent itself. They build simple nests of pebbles and often steal pebbles from the nests of other pairs.

Above: The Yellow-eyed Penguin digs its burrows beneath the trees in New Zealand's lush coastal forests. Like most penguins, it is very vocal – its Maori name is Hoiho, which literally means 'noise shouter'.

Opposite: Although most of us associate penguins with snow and ice, African Penguins breed in subtropical conditions with colonies often separated from the sea by beautiful white sand beaches.

lean years, however, the first chick to hatch is often the only one to survive. Unable to compete with its larger sibling, the second hatchling is muscled out when its parents do return with food and gradually starves to death.

Penguin chicks hatch covered with a fluffy layer of down and with their eyes firmly closed. Their eyes begin to open after three or four days but they keep their down for weeks or even months. For the first weeks of its life, a penguin chick is closely guarded by its parents. However, young penguins grow quickly and before long they are big enough to defend themselves from most winged predators. The smallest species reach near-adult size the fastest. Fairy Penguins may be left unguarded when they are as young as 15 days old. Most penguins, however, stay under the watchful eyes of their parents until they at least four weeks old.

Once they have reached a size at which they are deemed capable of being left alone by their parents, the downy youngsters of most species spend their time huddled together in crèches. These provide them with the protection of safety in numbers from the largest predatory birds and the benefit of other bodies against which to huddle for warmth in cold weather.

Right: King Penguins form large colonies that may contain several thousand individuals. The fluffy brown chicks, once they have reached a certain size, gather together in crèches while their parents search for food at sea.

Opposite: King Penguins do not build nests but incubate their eggs on their feet. The male and female take turns incubating, passing the egg between themselves when their partners return from the sea.

Above: Penguin colonies attract their fair share of winged predators. Here a King Penguin does its best to drive off a Brown Skua that has targeted its egg.

Burrowing and crevice-nesting penguin chicks are unusual in not forming crèches. Instead, they stay near the entrances of their protective nest chambers.

Freed from guard duty, both parents are now able to hunt at the same time, which is important if the growing chicks are to get enough food. This phase of a chick's life, known by biologists as the 'post-guarding phase', is the longest in its rearing, lasting from a month for the Fairy Penguin to over a year in the case of the King Penguin.

King Penguin chicks are unique in remaining dependent on their parents for food for so long. Most penguins, even Emperors, are ready to take to the sea and fend for themselves by the time they are four or five months old. A King Penguin's extended childhood is by no means easy, however. Living a year before fledging means surviving on land through the winter and, on the southerly islands where King Penguins breed, this constitutes one of the most extreme challenges faced by any animal.

During autumn, King Penguin chicks put on enormous quantities of fat and keep their shaggy coats of luxuriant down. Both of these help to keep them warm through the icy cold of the winter, most of which their parents spend at sea. The fat has an even more important role as a food store to keep them alive. During the winter, when food is scarce, the chicks are fed just four or five times by their parents. Some are not fed at all and are forced to fast right the way through to the spring.

If what King Penguin chicks go through seems hard, consider the fate of male Emperor Penguins. They survive the entire winter on Antarctica itself, enduring howling blizzards with winds of up to 125mph (200kph) and temperatures as low as –76°F (–60°C). What is more, they do this without feeding once and with nothing but the Aurora Australis and light from the moon and stars to illuminate the ice around them.

Emperor Penguins, like Kings, are too large to allow the breeding and raising of young in one brief southern summer. Rather than leave the chicks to take their chances, however, these birds have evolved another solution to the problem. Emperor Penguins pair up and mate during autumn, just as most other birds are leaving Antarctica. Courtship is relatively brief and, unlike most penguins, females often choose different partners every year.

Once she has laid her egg, the female passes it to the male and then turns her back on him and heads for the sea. The male then incubates the egg entirely on his own, balancing it on top of his feet where it is covered by a pocket of feathered skin to keep it warm. When the chick finally hatches two months later, the male feeds it on regurgitated liquid produced from the lining of his stomach until the female returns.

Opposite: Like King Penguins, Emperors incubate their eggs on their feet and they also keep their chicks there for as long as possible after hatching. By lifting its feet up off the ice this adult is both conserving body heat and preventing its chick from becoming too cold.

Below: Emperor Penguin chicks grow as large as their parents before losing their fluffy coats of down. Until they have fledged, they remain completely dependent on the adults for food.

During the two months of incubation through the bitter depths of the Antarctic winter, male Emperor Penguins may lose up to half their body weight. When their partners finally return to give the chick its first proper meal, they set off on the long trek over the sea ice to feed themselves. Once gorged, they return to feed the chicks and take over from their partners the job of keeping their youngsters warm.

The fact that male Emperor Penguins can survive the Antarctic winter at all seems little short of a miracle. No other animal on Earth spends so long in such bitter cold, let alone while fasting. They manage this incredible feat by huddling together to conserve heat and thus energy, each taking his turn on the outside of the group. A lone Emperor Penguin in this environment will lose 2lb (900g) of body weight every three days. By contrast, an Emperor Penguin in a huddle loses as little as 11oz (312g) over the same period. Taking turns at the edge of the group huddle is vital if all members are to survive and this itself is important, as the larger the group is, the more warmth it can conserve.

Once Emperor Penguin chicks have hatched, they grow quickly. By the height of summer, when food is most abundant, they are fully fledged and able to take to the sea and hunt for themselves.

Left: Female Emperor Penguins lay a single egg each year. Both parents work hard to find enough food to raise their chick, which grows to adulthood during the short Antarctic summer. During some feeding trips they may travel hundreds of miles from their colony.

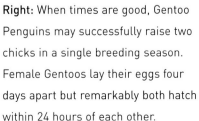

Right: When times are good, Gentoo Penguins may successfully raise two chicks in a single breeding season. Female Gentoos lay their eggs four days apart but remarkably both hatch within 24 hours of each other.

Emperor Penguin chicks form crèches from quite a young age. These are partly a way of defending themselves from predators but more importantly they help the young birds share their combined body heat to keep warm.

Penguin Habitats

A penguin's natural home is the sea. All penguins spend most of their lives in the water – their beautifully streamlined bodies are a testament to this fact. Most of the waters penguins inhabit are cold, either because of their geographical location or because of the direction of the currents that feed them. Even Galápagos Penguins, which live only a short distance south of the equator, swim and hunt in waters far cooler than the air above them. These cool, nutrient-rich waters well up from the ocean depths and are swept past the archipelago of the Galápagos Islands by the Cromwell Current.

Penguins are also more common near coasts than they are far out at sea. This is essentially a reflection of the abundance of their prey: krill, squid and small fish tend to concentrate in greater numbers over the continental shelf than in deeper, open ocean waters where nutrients are more scattered.

Penguins are supreme divers. Unlike most birds, which have hollow bones filled with a delicate honeycomb of struts for strength and lightness, penguins' bones are solid – built-in weight belts to help keep them submerged. Even at the surface, their bodies lie extremely low in the water. While most sea birds appear to sit on the waves, penguins lie under them with just their heads protruding. Their bodies float, but only just.

Although most penguins can dive to impressive depths in pursuit of prey, they spend most of their time in the upper few metres of the sea. When travelling in search of food or back to their breeding grounds, they swim just beneath the surface, occasionally leaping through it to catch a breath on the move.

Of course, penguins are not always swimming. They also rest at the surface, in between and following feeding dives, for example, and they sometimes even sleep while afloat.

The life of penguins at sea is undoubtedly more complex than we currently understand. Most observations of penguins in this environment are fleeting. Few people have spent much time following and directly studying them from the water.

Modern technology has provided some new insights into this major part of penguins' lives, however. Satellite tracking of birds fitted with transmitters at least tells us where they go, and provides other information, such as the

Right: Penguins seem unfazed by even the roughest seas. Their rotund bodies are surprisingly tough and they need to be, as these birds often find themselves bounced off rocks when trying to get out of the water.

duration of dives. We now know, for example, how far most species travel in search of food when they are not breeding. Even so, much more remains to be discovered than is currently known.

While the lives of penguins at sea are mysterious, their breeding colonies and lives on land have been studied in great detail. The fact that penguins cannot fly and are tolerant of humans almost to the point of complete disinterest makes them unusually easy to observe.

All the world's penguins are confined to the southern hemisphere but they breed on the shores of four continents. They also have colonies on dozens of islands, many around Antarctica but some much farther north.

The image most people have of penguins is as polar specialists and there are indeed species that breed surrounded by snow and ice. Perhaps

Above: Penguins are perfectly designed for life in the sea. Jumping from the water, or 'porpoising', is a technique which enables penguins both to take a breath and save energy when travelling near the surface, as air offers less resistance to their movement than water.

Above right: Being dark above and light below is a form of camouflage which helps hide penguins from both predators and prey in the water. This type of coloration is common among both marine animals and sea birds and is also prevalent among fish.

surprisingly, however, most penguins breed in places where the temperature is well above freezing – African Penguins even share beaches with sunbathing humans!

The most southerly breeders of all are the Adélie and Emperor Penguins. Most Adélie Penguins gather in colonies on Antarctica itself, arriving in October after spending the long southern winter at sea. Although they breed on the world's coldest continent, they avoid snowy shores and instead head for areas of ice-free barren rock where they build their low mound-shaped nests using small stones and pebbles. The briefness of the Antarctic summer forces Adélies to raise their chicks quickly and as a result they spend less time at their nesting colonies than any other penguins: a total of just four or five months of the year.

As we have already seen, Emperor Penguins get around the problem of the short Antarctic summer by incubating their eggs through the coldest months of the year. Unlike Adélies, Emperor Penguins gather and breed on the ice itself. In fact, most Emperor Penguins breed on sections of permanent sea ice, making them the only birds in the world never actually to set foot on land at all.

Two other penguin species have large colonies on Antarctica, the Chinstrap and the Gentoo. Both nest on the most northerly arm of the continent, the Antarctic Peninsula, which actually extends out of the Antarctic Circle. They also nest in great numbers on several islands farther north. Like the Adélie, Gentoo and Chinstrap Penguins choose areas of exposed rock for their colonies and fashion their nests from small stones. Chinstrap Penguins leave their colonies in May and spend the winter months at sea in waters north of the pack ice. Most Gentoos also winter at sea, although some birds remain at the more northerly breeding colonies throughout the year.

The world's second largest penguin, the King Penguin, breeds on islands in sub-Antarctic waters, from the Falklands eastward as far as Macquarie Island, directly southwest of New Zealand. It congregates in huge numbers on coastal plains, usually a short walk via a beach to the sea. By the beginning of autumn, the largest King Penguin colonies may contain more than a million birds. Like its close cousin the Emperor Penguin, the King Penguin incubates its egg on its feet and does not build a nest at all. As such, it is largely unrestricted in where it can breed, a fact that has undoubtedly contributed to its success as a species.

Two species of crested penguin share many of the islands that the King Penguin inhabits. The Rockhopper and the Macaroni Penguin both have a similarly sub-Antarctic distribution but desert their colonies in autumn, leaving the islands to the fluffy King Penguin chicks. Rockhopper Penguins also nest in southern Chile, around Cape Horn, on islands just south of New Zealand and right in the middle of the Atlantic Ocean on the island of Tristan da Cunha, which is on the same latitude as Buenos Aires. Macaroni Penguins, while not quite as widespread, also have colonies in Chile and farther south, with a few even nesting on the Antarctic Peninsula. The Macaroni is the world's most abundant penguin species, with a breeding population of almost 12 million pairs.

The other four crested penguin species have breeding colonies on and around New Zealand. The Royal Penguin nests only on Macquarie Island, but in large numbers and in 57 separate colonies. Far less common is the Snares Penguin, with a total population of around 70,000 birds. It is named after the Snares Islands, a small archipelago just 125 miles (200km) or so south of New Zealand that is covered with giant tree daisies, among which these small penguins nest.

The rarest of all crested penguins is the Fjordland Penguin, which actually breeds on New Zealand's South Island itself. It nests in dense temperate rain forests close to the shore, choosing sites beneath tree roots, under bushes or amongst boulders. The Fjordland Penguin is the least sociable of all the crested penguins, forming very loose colonies with pairs usually nesting out of sight of one another. On land, they are also unusually timid and are much more active at night than they are during the day.

Three other penguins nest in this part of the world. Erect-crested Penguins have colonies on the Antipodes and Bounty Islands to the southeast of New Zealand, and on the Auckland Islands farther west.

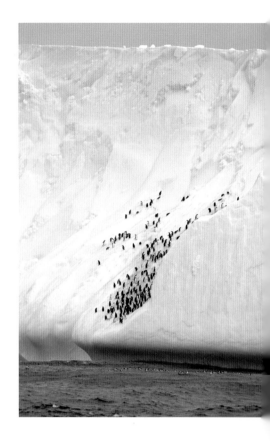

Above: Icebergs in the Antarctic are often vast, being formed from sections of the ice sheet itself, unlike those of the Arctic, which are mostly calved from glaciers.

Opposite above: It is not uncommon for different penguin species to gather together in areas where prey is abundant. Here Gentoos share the safety of an iceberg with Chinstraps in between forays for fish.

Opposite: King Penguin colonies are permanent affairs with many chicks staying at them through the winter. In some places, as here on South Georgia, they even span rivers.

The Yellow-eyed Penguin also nests on the Auckland Islands, as well as the Campbell Islands, Stewart Island and secluded parts of New Zealand's South Island. Unlike the six species of crested penguin, which winter at sea, the Yellow-eyed Penguin remains around its breeding sites throughout the year. It is the rarest of all penguins, with a world population that is estimated at fewer than 4000 individuals.

The Yellow-eyed Penguin is the fourth largest species after the Emperor, King and Gentoo. At the other end of the scale, but sharing some of the Yellow-eyed Penguin's breeding range, is the Fairy Penguin, little bigger than most species of duck. Fairy Penguins can be found right around New Zealand and are the only species to nest on the North Island as well as the South. They also have colonies right round Tasmania and are the only penguins to breed on the Australian mainland, being found along much of the southern coast. While Yellow-eyed Penguins like their space and hold small but individual nesting territories, Fairy Penguins are sociable breeders. Unlike their big neighbours, they dig nest burrows, generally about 7–10ft (2–3m) apart.

Fairy Penguins might be small in stature but they are far from short of self-confidence, sometimes nesting in close proximity to humans. The best-studied colony in Australia is in Sydney's North Harbour. They also nest around Perth and Hobart, the state capital of Tasmania.

Fairy Penguins are not unique in establishing colonies near where people live. African Penguins are even bolder, crossing beaches full of sunbathers and even entering people's gardens. Their most urban colony is at Boulder's Beach in Simon's Town, not far from Cape Town, South Africa's legislative

Left: Boulder's Beach, South Africa, is popular with people and penguins alike. In fact, the penguins have become something of a tourist attraction.

Opposite page: When they are not fishing at sea, African Penguins spend their time in large groups on the shore.

Above: Although the land is warm where African Penguins live, the waters offshore are quite cool. This is due largely to the influence of the northward-flowing Benguela Current, which brings nutrient-rich surface water all the way from the Southern Ocean around Antarctica.

capital. Here, they can be seen wandering along paved streets. Most African Penguins nest on offshore islands, however, where the risk of predation is lower. As well as in South Africa, they breed in Namibia and, at sea, are often spotted farther north, off Angola, Congo and Gabon.

African Penguins belong to the banded penguin group. On the other side of the Atlantic, the coasts of Argentina are home to Magellanic Penguins, their close relatives. Magellanic Penguins are the most southerly banded penguins, living and breeding as far south as Tierra del Fuego. Like other banded penguins though, they are really birds of temperate and tropical climes. In winter, Magellanic Penguins that nest on Atlantic shores migrate to waters off Brazil, while those that nest in Chile, facing the Pacific, migrate as far north as Peru.

Humboldt and Galápagos penguins are the most northerly penguins of all. Humboldt Penguins breed on the beaches and offshore islands of northern Chile and Peru. The southerly portion of their breeding range overlaps with the far northerly portion of that of Magellanic Penguins but elsewhere they have South America's Pacific beaches to themselves.

Galapágos Penguins are found only on the Galápagos Islands, which lie just south of the equator off the coast of Ecuador. Like Humboldt Penguins, they remain at their breeding colonies all year round, having a plentiful and constant supply of food right on their doorstep.

Above: In most places where they nest, Rockhoppers earn their name. They prefer rocky gullies overlooking the sea.

Right: This picture shows the route taken by Rockhoppers to one of their breeding sites in the Falkland Islands.

Emperor Penguins spend their lives either in or on water. The colonies
where they gather to breed are almost invariably situated on the floating
ice sheet that fringes the Antarctic continent proper. Male Emperor
Penguins are the only large creatures to spend the winter out on the
Antarctic ice. While the males huddle together in the bitter cold protecting
a single egg, the females travel great distances to the sea to feed.

Left: The Antarctic ice sheet is surrounded by mile after mile of floating pack ice. Outside the breeding season, this is the main haunt of Chinstrap Penguins. Chinstraps are the most abundant penguins in Antarctic waters in winter, far outnumbering all of the Emperors, Adélies and Gentoos that live there put together.

Penguin Predators

Penguins occupy the top half of the food chain. They hunt fish, squid and other animals to survive but they themselves fall victim to larger predators. On land or on ice, adult penguins are safe, but every time they enter the water they put themselves at risk.

In Antarctica, there is one predator that specializes in hunting penguins. Called the Leopard Seal, it feeds on little else. Leopard Seals hunt by stealth, lying in wait near the edge of the ice for penguins to enter or leave the water. They also sneak up on penguins from beneath, following their shadows as they walk over thin ice, then smashing through the surface to grab one unawares.

Leopard Seals are truly fearsome predators that have been known to attack and kill humans. Females, which are larger than males, sometimes reach 13ft (4m) in length and can weigh more than a third of a ton.

In Antarctic waters, penguin behaviour is strongly influenced by the presence of Leopard Seals. Adélie Penguins, which are particularly favoured prey, never linger on thin or broken ice but instead move across it as quickly as possible. They also make a point of standing back from the edge of the water – another favoured hunting technique of the Leopard Seal is to burst through the surface out onto the ice.

In the water, Leopard Seals lunge at penguins as they dive in at the start of fishing trips. From above, the seals are invisible, hidden, as they usually are, by the edge of the ice. This makes Antarctic penguins understandably nervous and explains why they almost invariably enter the water at speed and en masse.

Leopard Seals also hunt penguins returning from forays at sea. Adélies are picked out and grabbed in the water, but when hunting Emperor Penguins, Leopard Seals sometimes lurk on the ice. Emperor Penguins often use holes in the ice to get in and out of the sea and the powerful seals station themselves next to these, ready to grab their prey as it shoots from the water.

While Leopard Seals terrorize penguins around the Antarctic, other large pinnipeds use different methods to hunt them elsewhere. In the Falkland Islands, South American Sea Lions have been observed surging from the

Right: A young Fur Seal eyes a nesting Chinstrap Penguin. Fur Seals often kill and eat penguins, although they rarely attack them on land, preferring to hunt in the water where they are more agile.

surf to grab King Penguins from the beach. Also in the Falklands, Antarctic Fur Seals hunt penguins in gangs, chasing and killing them in the water. South of New Zealand, Hooker's Sea Lions hunt crested penguins in a similar way.

There are few places where penguins are safe from seals or sea lions. South American Fur Seals hunt them as far north as Peru, while the shores and islands of southern Africa are patrolled by Southern Sea Lions and South African Fur Seals. One predator, however, is ubiquitous and as much of a threat to seals and sea lions as to penguins – the Killer Whale.

Killer Whales have a virtually global distribution and there is nowhere where penguins nest or feed that they are not found. These mighty animals could be regarded the oceans' top predators: they hunt everything from shoaling fish to Blue Whales – they have even been known to hunt down and kill Great White Sharks.

Killer Whales seek out and tackle large prey by working co-operatively, but they seem to treat penguins almost like snacks. Pods of Killer Whales hang around in the waters just off penguin colonies and snap the birds up as they set off on feeding trips or return towards shore. Killer Whales have been known to play with their food, toying with a penguin like a cat with a mouse. Sometimes caught penguins are kept alive and released as practice prey for younger Killer Whales to help them learn to hunt. Live King

Above: A Galápagos Sea Lion thrashes a fish against the water to break it apart. Although fish make up the bulk of its diet, this species also hunts and kills Galápagos Penguins whenever the opportunity arises.

Above left: A bull South American Sea Lion lunges at Rockhopper Penguins in the Falkland Islands. Sea lions are formidable predators with fearsome canine teeth. Despite their obvious adaptations to life in the water, they can move surprisingly quickly on land.

Penguins have even been seen tossed skyward and batted through the air with a blow from a tail.

Although it is their natural home, the sea is a place of great peril for penguins. The waters close to shore are where danger is most heavily concentrated and birds tend to cross these areas at top speed to minimize the risk of attack. Penguins also show a great reluctance to enter the sea in small numbers – the bigger a group is, the better chance an individual within it has of avoiding predation. More pairs of eyes mean predators are more easily spotted and the swirl of moving bodies makes it harder for individual penguins to be picked out and chased down. In many Adélie colonies, crowds of penguins actually watch and wait for large groups of their own kind to return safely before diving into the water themselves, using them to show, literally, that the coast is clear.

It is ironic, given how clumsy they are on land, that land is the safest place for adult penguins to be. The Antarctic in particular has no large land-based predators and most penguins are big enough to repel any threat from the air. The same cannot be said for their eggs and chicks, however.

Below: A group of Leopard Seals rest on a slab of ice after a hard day's hunting. In the Antarctic, the Leopard Seal is penguin enemy number one, lying in wait for the birds as they enter and exit the water.

Gulls, skuas, petrels and other birds frequently make raids to steal the contents of penguins' nests, both hatched and unhatched. In the Falkland Islands and along the southern coasts of South America, they are joined by Striated Caracaras – land-based birds of prey. Anywhere where penguins nest on the mainland, they are at risk from small mammals. In South America, Gray Foxes and Geoffroy's Cats raid colonies, while in Africa mongooses are a major threat. The Fairy Penguins of Australia have their nests raided by reptiles in the shape of Tiger Snakes and Blue-tongued Lizards. Galápagos Penguin nests also suffer from attacks by snakes and even lose eggs to crustaceans – crimson-shelled Sally Lightfoot Crabs. Sadly, many of the worst nest-raiding pests are introduced. Rats and feral cats have devastated New Zealand's penguin colonies, for example.

Above: In many ways, sea lions are the mammalian equivalent of penguins, displaying similar adaptations to life in the sea. Their greater size, however, means that they are much more often enemies than competitors for food.

Right: The Killer Whale is one of the ocean's top predators. It has a wide-ranging diet which even extends to other whale species and Great White Sharks. It also includes most species of penguin.

Penguins of the World

When most of us think of penguins, we think of Antarctica. But while it is true that many penguins do live here, it is not the only place where they are found. Penguins inhabit most of the colder waters of the southern hemisphere and they follow fingers of cool, nutrient-rich surface water as far north as Africa and the shores of South America. There are even penguins on the Galápagos Islands, which are more famous for their finches and giant tortoises.

South American Penguins

The shores of South America and its islands are home to seven different species of penguin, three of them found nowhere else in the world. This is the stronghold of the banded penguins which, as a group, inhabit more northerly waters than their cousins.

The largest and by far the most common of the banded penguins is the Magellanic Penguin. An opportunist feeder, it hunts small fish, krill and squid in well-lit waters near the surface, rarely diving deeper than 165ft (50m) to find prey.

Magellanic Penguins breed around the southern tip of South America, including the Falkland Islands and Tierra del Fuego. They prefer to nest in burrows, which they excavate themselves, but also raise young on the surface where the ground is unsuitable for digging. Some Magellanic Penguin colonies are truly enormous, stretching over several miles. Most are used again and again, year after year, leaving whole sections of coastline honeycombed with burrows.

In winter, Magellanic Penguins leave their breeding colonies for warmer waters farther north. Some that nest in Argentina swim as far as Brazil. Pacific breeders spread north along Chile's coastline and into the waters off Peru.

Magellanic Penguin numbers have dropped in recent decades as increased catches made by fishing fleets have cut into their food supply. Nevertheless, they still exist around South America in their millions. Humboldt Penguins, their close relatives, have not fared so well.

Humboldt Penguins have a broad distribution along South America's Pacific coast, breeding from Algarrobo in Chile as far north as Isla Foca off Peru. They are named after the Humboldt Current, which wells up along this area of western South America. Like all upwelling systems, the Humboldt Current brings nutrients from the deep up into surface waters. These support a rich soup of plankton, which traditionally fed vast shoals of anchovies and other fish. Sadly, as a result of overfishing stocks of these have declined and so have the penguins which rely on them. Today, there are fewer than 20,000 Humboldt Penguins left.

Like their more southerly cousins, Humboldt Penguins like to burrow but will also nest on open ground. The shores along which they breed include some of the most arid terrain in the world and Humboldt Penguins

Right: Magellanic Penguins are by far the most common penguins around the coast of South America, occurring off Brazil, Uruguay, Argentina, Chile and Peru.

are unusual in being adapted to cope with heat rather than cold. Their faces have large areas of bare skin that are well supplied with blood vessels. These help the birds to stay cool in the heat of the day.

Just north of the Humboldt Penguin's range lie the shores of Ecuador. This country has no penguins of its own but the Galápagos Islands, which it governs, do. Like many of the creatures from this remarkable archipelago, Galápagos Penguins are found nowhere else in the world. They spend all year on and around the islands, breeding mainly on Fernandina and Isabela, which lie virtually on the equator.

Galápagos Penguins are the smallest and lightest coloured of the banded penguins, as well as the most tropical. Although the islands they live on are semi-arid and baked by the sun, the seas surrounding them are relatively cool. The Galápagos Islands are bathed by the upwelling waters of the Cromwell Current, which, like the Humboldt Current, is rich with nutrients from the deep. Ordinarily, this supports a wealth of marine life, but during El Niño years (occasions when an anomalous ocean current flows along the coast of Peru) it is blocked off and fish stocks plummet. Naturally, the creatures that feed on fish, including penguins, suffer. Galápagos Penguin

Above Rockhoppers have an extremely widespread distribution. There are three subspecies, one of which, shown here, nests around Cape Horn and the Falkland Islands.

Opposite: The Humboldt Penguin differs from the more common Magellanic by lacking a belly stripe. Sadly, it is now seriously threatened as a result of overfishing in the regions where it lives.

Above: The Macaroni Penguin breeds at the far south of Chile and Argentina. By far the largest colonies, however, are found on the island of South Georgia which lies 1300 miles (2090km) farther east.

Right: The Galápagos Penguin is the most northerly of all penguins, it lives almost on the equator. It is the smallest member of the banded penguin group.

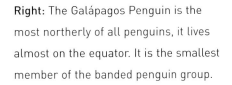

numbers are currently recovering from two extremely severe El Niños, one in 1982-83 and the other in 1997-98.

Galápagos Penguins are the second smallest of all penguins and by far the smallest South American species. The largest South American penguin, the King, can weigh ten times as much.

King Penguins breed on the Falkland Islands and several other islands farther east. They are much more oceanic birds than any of the banded penguins, often travelling long distances out to sea in search of food. King Penguin colonies are crowded, noisy places. This species' unusual breeding cycle means that they are continually occupied by fluffy brown chicks, although the adults spend most of the winter at sea.

The three other South American penguins breed on the Falkland Islands alongside the King. Gentoo Penguins form smaller colonies that rarely exceed a few hundred pairs. Unlike King Penguins, they actually build rudimentary nests and, in the Falklands and islands to the west on a similar latitude, remain at their colonies throughout the year.

Rockhopper Penguins and Macaroni Penguins live on the Falklands but also nest on South America proper, in southern Chile and Argentina. Their colonies can be enormous, each containing several hundred thousand pairs. Rockhoppers are the smallest of the crested penguins and the most widespread. As well as in South America, they breed on islands south of New Zealand, and on most of the other specks of land that lie in between. Macaroni Penguins, although not quite so widespread as Rockhoppers, are even more numerous with a global population of well over 25 million, more than any other penguin species.

Above: Trapped on land until they fledge, King Penguin chicks spend the winter at their colonies, protected from the cold by their fluffy coats of down.

Opposite: Most of the places where King Penguins breed are free from snow in spring and summer. Likewise, the waters in which they hunt are usually free of ice.

Left: Gentoo Penguins are found in both icy and warmer waters. As well as breeding on Antarctica, they have colonies on most of the sub-Antarctic islands, including the Falklands.

Left: The Macaroni is one of the larger crested penguins with a thickset body and a distinctive bright red bill. These Macaroni Penguins are at the edge of a colony in South Georgia.

African Penguins

Most people are amazed when they first hear that there are penguins in Africa. The idea that birds they normally associate with icebergs can live on its sun-drenched beaches just seems too bizarre. But they do.

In fact, Africa is home to just one species of penguin – the African Penguin – which is found nowhere else. One of the four species of banded penguins, they evolved here and are perfectly suited to the conditions in which they find themselves. They cope with the heat by spending most of the day in their nest burrows or in the sea. If they do find themselves stuck in the open, they pant to cool down.

African Penguins breed in the countries of South Africa and Namibia. A few populations have their colonies on the mainland but most nest on sandy islands out in the sea. Wherever they breed, African Penguins face attacks on their nests from Kelp Gulls and Sacred Ibises. On the mainland, mongooses and genets also raid their nests, and the adults are sometimes killed and eaten by leopards.

The distribution of African Penguins is tied closely to the Benguela Current, which sweeps past Africa's southwestern tip. This current starts its life in the Southern Ocean and carries cold, nutrient-rich water northward. Off South Africa and Namibia it meets the warm, south-flowing Agulhas Current and the two mix, creating ideal conditions for the growth of plankton, which supports a wealth of marine life.

African Penguins feed mainly on shoaling fish, particularly anchovies, sardines, horse mackerel and round herrings. These staples are supplemented by squid and crustaceans. Most food is caught in shallow water during dives that last for just two or three minutes, although occasionally African Penguins will plunge down to 330ft (100m) or more to chase prey. Lengths of feeding trips vary depending on the local abundance of food. When times are good, round trips of 20 miles (32km) or less are common, but when fish are scarcer, African Penguins sometimes travel up to 70 miles (110km). Generally speaking, forays are shortest when penguins have chicks to feed.

Living in a warm climate has certain advantages. For instance, unlike most of their counterparts elsewhere, African Penguins can breed all year round. That said, there are peak breeding times for colonies, which coincide

Right: Africa is home to just one penguin species. African Penguins belong to the banded penguin group. Like most penguins, they are very inquisitive.

Above: Superficially, African Penguins are very similar to Magellanic Penguins, which live at a similar latitude on the other side of the Atlantic Ocean.

Opposite: The orange light of sunrise bathes an African Penguin as it returns from the sea. African Penguins are also known as jackass penguins because of their loud braying call.

with seasonal gluts of food. In Namibia, breeding activity is most intense during December and January. In South Africa the peak comes a bit later, running from March to May.

African Penguin chicks are guarded by their parents until they are about 30 days old. Once they have reached this age, both parents must hunt most of the time in order to feed them adequately and they are left in crèches while the adults are at sea. Fledging can take anything from two to four months, depending on the availability and quality of food. Once they have fledged, the young penguins take to the sea, returning to their colonies a year or more later to moult into their adult plumage.

All African Penguins moult once a year. During this time they are unable to swim and hunt for food, so it is important that they put on weight before the process begins. Moulting takes around 20 days to complete and adults can lose almost half of their body weight during this period. As soon as they are able to re-enter the sea, they do so and they remain there for about six weeks, hunting almost continuously to fatten themselves up again.

Left: African Penguins live and breed on the coast of South Africa and on the offshore islands. Most will spend their lives in the same colony, although a few disperse to join other colonies as juveniles. Most breeding pairs stay together for consecutive seasons and some have been know to remain together for over ten years.

Penguins of Antarctica

Antarctica is the coldest place on Earth. In winter, the sun disappears completely for two months. Fierce blizzards lash the landscape, driven by winds gusting up to 125mph (200kph). Temperatures drop to a mind-numbing −76°F (−60°C).

To imagine these conditions is hard enough. Actually to be able to live in them is astounding. Male Emperor Penguins do this every winter and they do it without food. On their feet they carry a precious cargo, a single egg which they incubate there until spring.

Emperor Penguins are the largest penguins of all and one of five species that breed and bring up their young on Antarctica and its surrounding islands. The other four, the Macaroni, Adélie, Gentoo and Chinstrap Penguins, incubate their eggs and raise their chicks to fledging in the short spring and summer. They leave the frozen continent in autumn and spend the winter at sea.

Emperor Penguins are clearly made of strong stuff but even they would not survive an Antarctic winter alone. That fact that they do survive is down to an incredible example of co-operative behaviour that has very few parallels in the natural world. Unrelated males, each with its own egg to protect, work together. They huddle for warmth and protection from the gales and, in doing so, save not only their own lives but those of the next generation of chicks.

Each male takes his turn on the edge of the huddle before moving back in. This behaviour appears almost intelligent, as if the birds know they each have to take a shift bearing the brunt of the weather if they are all to survive. It is, however, an amazing example of apparent group behaviour resulting from the reactions of individuals to the physical conditions in which they find themselves. As they reach the edge of the group, individual male Emperors start to cool down. However, it is only when they start to feel too cold that they move, peeling off from the windward side of the huddle and waddling down the flanks to the lee. As they leave, the individuals they were shielding become the new windward edge. When they in turn move around to the lee, those that got there before them find themselves back in the huddle again.

Right: The Emperor is the most Antarctic penguin of all, breeding only on the ice sheet surrounding the continent itself. Although other penguins breed on Antarctica, they all also have colonies on islands farther north.

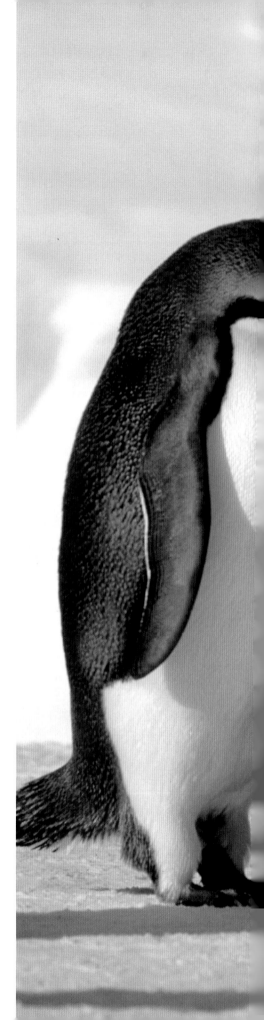

Female Emperors leave the males to spend the worst of the winter at sea. When they return, two months later, the sea ice is still thick and they have a long trek to make before they finally reach their partners and chicks.

As the ice retreats and the chicks grow, the adults spend more and more time in the water, hunting both for themselves and their young. It is at about this time that Antarctica's other penguins begin to return to the continent, picking their way through the drift ice to their colonies by the sea.

The most southerly travellers are Adélie Penguins, which nest along shores around most of Antarctica, including the bite taken out of it known as the Ross Sea. Like Emperors, Adélie Penguins are truly Antarctic birds, nesting almost exclusively on the continent itself. Their breeding cycle is swift, taking less than five months from mating to fledging of the chicks. This enables them to make the most of the short Antarctic summer and ensures that all birds are independent and can look after themselves before the sea ice reasserts its grip along the shores.

Above: The Macaroni Penguin is the only crested penguin to nest on Antarctica. It feeds on a wide range of prey, taking krill, fish and small squid. This fact, combined with its ability to tolerate a wide range of water temperatures, makes it the most successful and abundant of all penguin species.

Opposite: Adélie Penguin numbers are higher today than they were in the past, due largely to decreased competition for krill from baleen whales, which were decimated in previous centuries by hunting.

Chinstrap Penguins nest on the Antarctic Peninsula and islands surrounding the continent. They are particularly common on the South Sandwich Islands, where more than 10 million of them nest – just under two-thirds of the global population.

Chinstraps are the world's second most abundant penguins. They breed in rocky areas and build nests from small pebbles. They often choose lofty sites for their colonies as these are the first to become free of snow, increasing the amount of time they have to raise their chicks.

Unlike Emperor Penguins, which are squid specialists, Chinstrap Penguins feed mainly on krill and small fish. They rarely travel far from their colonies to find food, searching instead for it among the pack ice close to shore. Those that nest on Antarctica leave for the winter, but most of those farther north stay around their colonies throughout the year.

Above: Chinstraps are the smallest of the Antarctic penguins. They breed in vast colonies. The largest of these, on the South Sandwich Islands, is estimated to contain more than 10 million birds – a population greater than that of Los Angeles or London.

Above: By the end of summer most Gentoos have put on weight and are quite rotund. The fat beneath their skin works both as a food store and an insulating coat. Gentoos that breed on Antarctica head north with the advancing ice in autumn.

Gentoos are the largest of the brush-tailed penguins and the second largest penguins to nest on Antarctica. Like Chinstraps, they have colonies on the Antarctic Peninsula and the South Sandwich Islands, but they also nest on several islands farther north. Gentoo Penguins are unusual in that they frequently move their colonies, rarely staying in one spot for more than a few years. Compared with most penguins, they are fairly agile on land and often site their nests a mile or more from the sea.

The fifth Antarctic penguin is the world's most common, the Macaroni. It nests on the Antarctic Peninsula but is more abundant on the string of islands that circle the continent, several hundred miles north of its shores. Macaronis have a varied diet, catching fish, squid and krill. They do most of their hunting by day but occasionally forage at night, restricting their dives to no more than 20ft (6m) below the surface.

Emperor Penguins are able to withstand conditions that would kill most other creatures. Their sociable nature and willingness to share body heat enables them to survive the worst weather that the Antarctic can throw at them. Emperor Penguin chicks hatch in July at the end of the Antarctic winter. Six months later they fledge and make their way to the sea.

Penguins of Australia and New Zealand

Australasia has some fantastic wildlife. New Zealand in particular is home to many wonderful birds which evolved there and are found nowhere else in the world. Among New Zealand's unique avifauna are two species of penguin, the Yellow-eyed and the Fjordland. Both are rare and unusual in that they nest in forests, their loose colonies scattered beneath the boughs of gnarled rainforest trees.

As a nation, New Zealand has a very small population and its South Island, where these penguins breed, is even more sparsely populated than the North. Unfortunately, however, mammals other than humans have made it their home: rats and feral cats brought over by European settlers wander the mossy rainforests unchecked. Over the decades, they have caused havoc to New Zealand's ground-nesting native birds, including its penguins.

The Yellow-eyed Penguin is the largest to nest anywhere in this region and is the only member of its genus. It has the unfortunate distinction of being the world's rarest penguin, with a population of under 4000 birds. These are spread over six different colonies, three on South Island and the others on smaller islands offshore.

The Yellow-eyed Penguin is not much of a traveller – adults spend their lives in or around the nesting colonies, which can be half a mile or more inland. Newly fledged chicks wander farther during their first year at sea but return to the colonies as soon as they are old enough to breed.

Like most penguins, the Yellow-eyed Penguin is relatively long-lived – the majority of birds that make it to adulthood survive until they are at least 20 years old. Even by penguin standards, Yellow-eyed Penguins are extremely faithful partners. Couples stay together and raise chicks year after year. Generally speaking, these penguins only seek out new mates if their old partner dies. Yellow-eyed Penguins are unfussy eaters, feeding on a wide range of fish and squid. They do most of their hunting within a few miles of their breeding colonies, diving up to 400ft (120m) as many as 200 times a day to catch their prey.

Fjordland Penguins nest on Stewart Island and the southwestern coast of New Zealand's South Island, a place of forested cliffs and sea-flooded valleys. They are the most timid of all crested penguins. Unlike Yellow-eyed Penguins, adult Fjordlands leave their colonies for part of the southern

Right: With their pale, almost white feet, Rockhopper Penguins look even more smartly turned out than most as they return from the sea.

winter, returning in June to begin courtship and breeding. The chicks fledge when they are just 10 weeks old and then take to the sea, coming back to the colonies five years later, when they are finally ready to breed.

Because of the isolation and rugged nature of their habitat, Fjordland Penguins have been little studied. Not much is known about their diet and their total population has never been accurately measured. What is known is that they are rare, with possibly as few as 3000 breeding pairs.

If Yellow-eyed and Fjordland Penguins are emblematic of the problems faced by New Zealand's endemic birds, Fairy Penguins are a case of success in adversity. These tiny penguins breed right around New Zealand's coast and are found in even larger numbers around Tasmania and on Australia's southern shores. The world population is well over a million birds.

Fairy Penguins are homebodies that rarely stray far from their colonies. Most nest in burrows, which they excavate themselves in sand, soil or amongst vegetation. In a few places, they use caves or crevices between fallen rocks. Fairy Penguins seem to have little fear of people and a few nest in urban areas. One population in Victoria has colonized a breakwater originally built for the 1956 Olympic Games.

Above: Mutual preening helps penguin partners reaffirm their pair bond and also rids them of any ticks or other parasites they may have picked up on the nest. These are Yellow-eyed Penguins, which are native to New Zealand and its offshore islands.

Right: Four Fairy Penguins scramble across North Curl Beach near Sydney, Australia. This is quite an unusual sight as they are rarely seen out of their burrows or the sea during daylight hours. Fairy Penguins are sometimes called Blue Penguins because of their distinctive coloration.

Below: The Fjordland Penguin is both endangered and relatively little known. It nests in the forests of southwestern New Zealand, scrambling across rocky beaches to get from the sea to its breeding grounds. Like many of New Zealand's flightless birds, its numbers have plummeted since the accidental introduction of rats and feral cats by European settlers.

The world's smallest penguins, Fairy Penguins are also known as Blue Penguins, for obvious reasons. Unusually, the juveniles have almost identical plumage to the adults. The clean lines seen between the back and belly feathers in other species, while still there, are less obvious, especially from distance. Rather, the two colours, slate-blue and pure white, appear to merge.

Fairy Penguins mainly hunt small fish. They spend the day at sea or in their burrows, only venturing across land at dawn or dusk. For this reason they are rarely seen by people, despite their abundance. They are often heard, however, as they are very vocal birds. At night, their colonies can create quite a racket, echoing to the sound of various trills, brays and whistles. Fairy Penguins also bark to keep contact at sea.

There are three other penguin species unique to Australasia, although none nest on Australia or New Zealand proper. All three are types of crested penguin. By far the most abundant is the Royal Penguin, which nests only on Macquarie Island, an Australian protectorate roughly halfway between Tasmania and Antarctica. The Royal Penguin is the largest of all the crested penguins and the only one with a white face. Although restricted to one island for breeding, it ranges widely at sea in the winter. In spring, almost

two million Royal Penguins return to Macquarie Island, cramming themselves into 57 chaotic colonies.

Slightly smaller than the Royal Penguin, the Erect-crested Penguin breeds to the southeast of New Zealand on two archipelagoes – the Antipodes and the Bounty Islands. It too is numerous, with an estimated population of around a million birds.

The Snares Penguin is rarer, with a breeding population of around 33,000 pairs. This number is quite stable and is a reflection, more than anything, of the small size of its breeding sites. The Snares Islands, after which it is named, are the only places on which it has established colonies and they have a combined area of just 620 acres (250ha).

Australasia's other penguin in the only one also found outside the region – the Rockhopper. It shares Macquarie Island and the Antipodes with its larger relatives, the Royal and Erect-crested Penguins, and nests alongside the Yellow-eyed Penguin on Campbell Island and the Aucklands, directly south of New Zealand.

Most Rockhopper colonies are enormous and densely packed, with as many as three nests per square yard. They tend to be situated in steep gullies close to the sea. The name Rockhopper is very appropriate, as journeys to and from the nests usually involve a fair amount of jumping and climbing over boulders and scree.

Above: The Snares Penguin nests on the Snares Islands just to the south of New Zealand. It is similar in appearance to the very closely related Fjordland Penguin, which differs in appearance by having a slightly lighter yellow crest and a small patch of white feathers on its face.

Left: The Erect-crested Penguin, like its smaller relative the Rockhopper Penguin, has bright red eyes and a stubby dark orange beak. It has a much smaller range, however, with breeding populations on just a few islands south of New Zealand.

Below: Royal Penguins huddle between clumps of tussock grass. The entire world population of around two million Royal Penguins nests on one speck of land in the far southwest of the Pacific Ocean, Macquarie Island, which is an Australian protectorate.

Penguin Directory

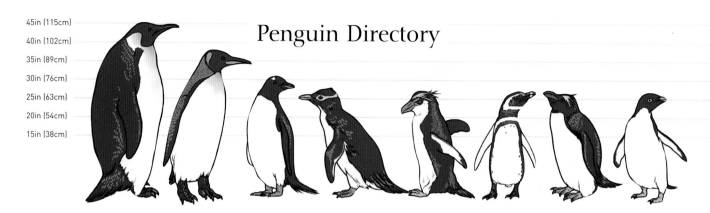

45in (115cm)
40in (102cm)
35in (89cm)
30in (76cm)
25in (63cm)
20in (54cm)
15in (38cm)

Species	Emperor Penguin	King Penguin	Gentoo Penguin	Yellow-eyed Penguin	Royal Penguin	Magellanic Penguin	Macaroni Penguin	Adélie Penguin
Latin name	Aptenodytes forsteri	Aptenodytes patagonicus	Pygoscelis papua	Megadyptes antipodes	Eudyptes schlegeli	Spheniscus magellanicus	Eudyptes chrysolophus	Pygoscelis adeliae
Subspecies	None	A. p. patagonicus and A. p. halli	P. p. papua and P. p. ellsworthii	None	None	None	None	None
Average length	45in (115cm)	37.5in (95cm)	31in (78cm)	28.5in (72cm)	27.5in (70cm)	27.5in (70cm)	27.5in (70cm)	27.5in (70cm)
Weight range	55-84lb (25-38kg)	26.5-35.25lb (12-16kg)	10.25-14.25lb (4.6-6.5kg)	9.25-18.75lb (4.2-8.5kg)	9-18lb (4-8kg)	8.25-14.25lb (3.75-6.5kg)	8-14lb (3.6-6.4kg)	8.5-11.75lb (3.9-5.3kg)
Distinguishing features	Large size, orange ear spots and yellow bib	Large size; back lighter grey than that of the Emperor Penguin and ear patches more orange	White 'eyebrows' forming a band across the top of the head; brush tail and largely orange bill	Yellow eyes and a yellow band of feathers reaching across the top of the head	Yellow crest and large orange bill; the only crested penguin with a white face	Dark band around chest and belly; dark feathers from the back extend in a collar around the front of the neck; patch of white at the base of the bill	Black face and wispy yellow crest sprouting from the front of the head	All black head and short, stubby bill; white ring around the eye
Population	400,000	2.5 million	700,000	Fewer than 4000	2 million	1.8 million	At least 24 million	6 million
Number of eggs	1	1	2	2	2	2	2	2
Incubation period	64-67 days	Around 55 days	Around 34 days	39-51 days	30-40 days	Around 40 days	Around 35 days	30-40 days
Breeding range	Mainland Antarctica	Cape Horn eastward to Macquarie Island – none south of 60 degrees	Antarctic Peninsula and most sub-Antarctic islands	Stewart, Auckland and Campbell Islands, off southern New Zealand	Macquarie Island	Southern Argentina, Tierra del Fuego, Chile and the Falkland Islands	Antarctic Peninsula and most sub-Antarctic islands	Mainland Antarctica and a few sub-Antarctic islands
Distribution at sea	Southern Ocean	Southern Ocean, South Atlantic and Southern Indian Ocean	Southern Ocean, South Atlantic and southern Indian Ocean	Far southwest Pacific Ocean, south of New Zealand	Far southwest of the Pacific and far southeast of the Indian Ocean	Far southwest of the Atlantic and far southeast of the Pacific	Southern Ocean, South Atlantic, far southeastern Pacific and southern Indian Ocean	Southern Ocean
Diet	Mainly squid and fish, with some krill	Mainly squid and fish, with some krill	Krill and other crustaceans, fish and squid	Mainly fish, with some squid	Mainly fish, with some krill and squid	Fish, krill and squid	Krill, fish and squid	Mainly krill, with some small fish and squid
Maximum diving depth	1870ft (565m)	1065ft (325m)	696ft (212m)	400ft (120m)	164ft (50m)	295ft (90m)	262ft (80m)	574ft (175m)
Average swimming speed	Up to 5-7.5mph (8.5-12km/h)	4.5mph (7.5km/h)	3.75mph (6km/h)	Unknown	Unknown	4.5mph (7.5km/h)	4.5mph (7.5km/h)	4.5mph (7.5km/h)
Predators	Leopard Seal, Antarctic Fur Seal, Killer Whale	South American Sea Lion, South American Fur Seal, Antarctic Fur Seal, Sub-Antarctic Fur Seal, Killer Whale	Leopard Seal, South American Sea Lion, South American Fur Seal, Antarctic Fur Seal, Sub-Antarctic Fur Seal, Killer Whale	New Zealand Sea Lion, New Zealand Fur Seal, Killer Whale, sharks	New Zealand Sea Lion, New Zealand Fur Seal, Killer Whale, sharks	South American Sea Lion, South American Fur Seal, Killer Whale, sharks	Leopard Seal, South American Sea Lion, South American Fur Seal, Antarctic Fur Seal, Sub-Antarctic Fur Seal, Killer Whale	Leopard Seal, Antarctic Fur Seal, Sub-Antarctic Fur Seal, Killer Whale
Average lifespan	20 years	20 years	15 years	15 years	10 years	16 years	12 years	16 years
Status	Stable	Stable and increasing	Stable	Endangered	Stable	In gradual decline due to overfishing	Stable and increasing	Stable

	African Penguin	Chinstrap Penguin	Erect-crested Penguin	Humboldt Penguin	Snares Penguin	Fjordland Penguin	Rockhopper Penguin	Galápagos Penguin	Fairy Penguin
	Spheniscus demersus	*Pygoscelis antarctica*	*Eudyptes sclateri*	*Spheniscus humboldti*	*Eudyptes robustus*	*Eudyptes pachyrhynchus*	*Eudyptes chrysocome*	*Spheniscus mendiculus*	*Eudyptula minor*
	None	None	None	None	None	None	E. c. chrysocome, E. c. filholi and E. c. moseleyi	None	E. m. albosignata, E. m. chathamensis, E. m. iredalei, E. m. minor, E. m. novaehollandiae and E. m. variabilis
	27.5in (70cm)	27in (68.5cm)	26.5in (67cm)	25.5in (65cm)	22in (56cm)	21.5in (55cm)	21.5in (55cm)	21in (53cm)	16.5in (42cm)
	5.25-9lb (2.4-4kg)	7.5-11lb (3.4-5kg)	6.5-14lb (2.9-6.35kg)	7.75-13lb (3.5-5.9kg)	5.75-9.5lb (2.6-4.3kg)	5.5-10.75lb (2.5-4.9kg)	5-10lb (2.3-4.5kg)	3.75-5.75lb (1.7-2.6kg)	1.75-3lb (0.8-1.3kg)
	Similar to Magellanic Penguin but lacks dark collar and white patch at the base of the bill	White face with a thin 'strap' of dark feathers extending under the chin	Spectacular light yellow, brush-like crests – the largest of any crested penguin – reaching from the top of the beak to the back of the head	Patch of bare skin at the base of the bill; no dark collar or band around the chest and belly	Neat yellow crests extending from the top of the bill to the back of the head; spot of white at the base of the bill, where the two mandibles meet	Superficially similar to the Snares Penguin but has a broken patch of white feathers beneath each eye	The smallest crested penguin with the stubbiest bill; yellow feathers of 'eyebrows' appear split from the rest of those in each crest	Collar poorly defined and dark spots scattered on the belly; little white on the face compared with other banded penguins	Small size and almost blue feathers on its back and the top of its head; piercing silvery-grey eyes with clearly defined pupils
	200,000	18 million	800,000	Under 20,000	70,000	7000–10,000	7 million	10,000	1.2 million
	2	2	2	2	2	2	2	2	2
	Around 40 days	Around 37 days	Around 35 days	40-42 days	31-37 days	30-36 days	Around 33 days	38-40 days	33-39 days
	South Africa, Namibia and nearby islands	The Antarctic Peninsula and sub-Antarctic islands	Antipodes, Bounty and Auckland Islands	Chile and Peru	Snares Islands, off southern New Zealand	Southwestern coast of New Zealand's South Island, and nearby Stewart Island	Islands right around Antarctica, between the latitudes of 37 and 53 degrees south	Galápagos Islands	Southern Australia, Tasmania, New Zealand and offshore islands
	Southeastern Atlantic and far southwest of the Indian Ocean	Southern Ocean and far south of the Atlantic, Pacific and Indian Oceans	Far southwest of the Pacific Ocean	Distribution at sea. Offshore waters near breeding colonies, following the Humboldt Current	Far southwest of the Pacific Ocean	Far southwest of the Pacific Ocean	Southern Atlantic, Pacific and Indian Oceans	Waters immediately surrounding the Galápagos archgipelago	Waters near its breeding colonies
	Small fish and, less commonly, squid	Mainly krill, with some small fish	Fish and krill	Small fish, squid and crustaceans	Mainly krill, with some squid and small fish	Mainly squid, with some crustaceans and small fish	Mainly krill, other crustaceans and some small fish	Small fish and crustaceans	Small fish and squid
	427ft (130m)	587ft (179m)	Unknown	174ft (53m)	Unknown	Unknown	551ft (168m)	105ft (32m)	226ft (69m)
	3mph (5km/h)	5.25mph (8.5km/h)	Unknown	3mph (5km/h)	Unknown	Unknown	4.5mph (7.5km/h)	Unknown	4.25mph (7km/h)
	Cape Fur Seal, Killer Whale, sharks	Leopard Seal, Antarctic Fur Seal, Sub-Antarctic Fur Seal, Killer Whale	New Zealand Sea Lion, New Zealand Fur Seal, Killer Whale, sharks	South American Fur Seal, South American Sea Lion, Killer Whale, sharks	New Zealand Sea Lion, New Zealand Fur Seal, Killer Whale, sharks	New Zealand Sea Lion, New Zealand Fur Seal, Killer Whale, sharks	South American Sea Lion, South American Fur Seal, Sub-Antarctic Fur Seal, New Zealand Sea Lion, New Zealand Fur Seal, Killer Whale, sharks	Galápagos Sea Lion, Galápagos Fur Seal, sharks	Australian Sea Lion, New Zealand Sea Lion, New Zealand Fur Seal, sharks
	11 years	13 years	Unknown	16 years	Unknown	Unknown	10 years	Unknown	7 years
	Vulnerable	Stable	Stable	Threatened	Stable	Threatened	Stable	Endangered	Stable

Index

Picture Credits

© Corbis:
Theo Allofs/Corbis: 19, 66-67, 69 (above), 85.
Tom Brakefield/Corbis: 16 (below), 28 (left), 62-63.
John Conrad/Corbis: 38.
Tim Davis/Corbis: 8-9, 22-23, 25 (above), 29, 39, 42-43, 64-65, 80-81, 83, 86-87.
David Gray/Reuters/Corbis: 91 (above).
Martin Harvey, Gallo Images/Corbis: 76.
Jon Hicks/Corbis: 50-51 (centre).
Gallo Images/Corbis: 33 (above), 74-75.
Peter Johnson/Corbis: 56-67, 60 (left).
Wolfgang Kaehler/Corbis: 10, 20-21, 30-31, 34, 40-41, 52-53, 58-59, 68, 69 (below right), 82, 84, 88-89, 92, 93 (below).
Joe McDonald/Corbis: 36.

Rick Price/Corbis: 6-7, 12-13.
Kevin Schafer/Corbis: 2-3, 18 (above), 26-27, 33 (below), 35, 44-45, 71, 90.
Paul A. Souders/Corbis: 14-15, 37 (left), 72-73.
Keren Su/Corbis: 46-47.
Roger Tidman/Corbis: 78-79.
Onne van der Wal/Corbis: 10-11 (below).
Winfred Wisniewski, Frank Lane/Corbis: 54-55.

© iStockphoto.com:
Giovanni Antico: 50 (left).
Graham Bedingfield: 77.
Nick Byrne: 5 (centre,) 8.
Pete Favelle: 48.
Torsten Karock: 51 (right).
Andrea Leone: 47 (right).
Stephen Martin 93 (above).
Nancy Nehring: 28 (right), 60 (right).

Thomas O'Neil: 5 (above), 32.
Chris Oxendine: 24 (above).
Vladimir Pomortsev: 69 (below left).
Patrick Roherty: 37 (right), 49 (below), 52 (left).
Dennis Sabo: 62.
Wolfgang Schoenfield: 27 (right), 61, 70 (above).
Silense: 5 (below).
Vance Smith: 24-25 (below).
Jose Tejo: 49 (above).
Geoff Whiting: 16 (above).
Neil Wigmore: 34 (below).
Jan Will: 17 (left).

© Tracy Rich/ARWP Ltd: 1, 11 (above), 17 (right), 18 (below), 41 (right), 70 (below).

© Simon Meeds: 91 (below).